Magpie Tales

SB Wright

Magpie Tales
Copyright SB Wright ©2017

Cover Image: A. Broughton-Wright
Cover Design: Vivid Covers
Layout & Typset: Close-Up Books

All rights reserved. No part of this book may be reproduced in any form by any electronic or mechanical means including photocopying, recording, or information storage and retrieval without permission in writing from the authors.

ISBN-978-0-9876232-6-3

Published by Close-Up Books
Melbourne, Australia

For Alison

Acknowledgements

Many of the poems in this collection first appeared at www.sbwrightpoet.blogspot.com.au but additional pieces also appeared in the following publications:

Tincture Journal, Verity La, Snap Literary Journal, Writ Poetry Review, Pressure Gauge Journal, Bluepepper, Poetry and Place Anthology 2015, A Hundred Gourds Journal, 50 Haikus Issue 5, Volume 1, IN Daily Adelaide's Independent News and *Eureka Street*.

Thanks to the editors of the above publications for their support.

Contents

Rural Mythologies- Part I

8	*midday heat*
9	*That Summer*
11	*Beach landing*
13	*silk flowers*
14	*Crossroads*
15	*Black Snake Driving*
17	*limestone ruins*
18	*A Shepherd Mourning*
20	*Airport Lounge Remembrance*
21	*outliving*
22	*Lest We Forget*
24	*blackbirds*
25	*Those Country Towns*
27	*old farm midden*
28	*A Rural Mythology*

Wild Dogs Dreaming- Part II

30	*The King*
32	*morning chill*
33	*Lucilia Cuprina - an ode.*
34	*First Carvings*
36	*blistered*
37	*Wild Dogs Dreaming*
38	*A Fox Thought*

39	*The Bull and the China pieces*
40	*Confusion and Showgirl Tunes*
41	*Unguarded*
42	*eating twilight*

Notes

Rural Mythologies

midday heat
      the water song
           of magpies

That Summer

That summer saw me four foot high;
A desert ratbag caked in grime.
Ten years of rain-less pale blue sky
Made magical our swimming time.

Another ratbag caked in grime,
My brother scaled sheer ochre cliffs;
Magician of our swimming time,
He birdlike caught the thermal lifts.

My brother scaled sheer ochre cliffs;
A moment saw him act a fool.
He birdlike caught the thermal lift
Before he speared the desert pool.

A moment saw him act a fool.
My breath caught in my thumping chest,
Before he speared the desert pool.
A right of passage; threshold met.

My breath I held in thumping chest,
Each time he dove to best them all.
A right of passage, a threshold met
Until the ripples slowly lulled.

Each time he dove, he beat them all
And none could say he'd failed the test;
Until the ripples slowly lulled
And our hearts knew what minds had guessed.

And none would say he'd failed the test
But magic died that summer day.
Our hearts knew well what minds had guessed
When foolish games led boys astray.

The magic died that summer day;
Tears filled the rain-less pale blue sky.
When foolish games led boys astray,
The summer saw me four foot high.

Beach landing
after R Somerton

We wait until low tide.
Wade to the island,
rifles slung crossways
in case we fall.
The beach a 10 foot crawl
through mangrove mud.

The stink hits us
half way out,
wind blowing from the south
the smell of the dead and dying
fish mixed with the mess
of a thousand Shags.

On some silent cue,
we unsling,
slide in the longs.
We line them up in twos or threes.
Work like machines;
score a century each, maybe more.
Wade back before the tide
to weathered smiles of fishermen
and a crate of King George.

Later, discharged
with one working leg,
I ask him what it was like.

He shakes his head.
Stares instead
at the island.

each year
silk flowers by the road
on the same day

Crossroads

Our grand farmhouse stands at the crossroads of town that is no more. Only stone buildings remain – us and the old hall. The family that built the house were immigrants seeking freedom from religious troubles and the whims of petty kings in Central Europe. They brought with them new notions of faith and built things to last.

Clearing the Bridal Creeper from the Honeysuckle hedge one year, we came across an old beer bottle placed "just so" at its base. It put me in mind of a placation, to spirits or old household gods because even new faith carries old baggage.

> dancehall tunes
> shadows drink at the lights edge

The mayor, a descendant, laughed and told us of the old bylaw that said alcohol couldn't be taken within 200 yards of the hall.

Black Snake Driving

We drive
north to the next town;
pass fields of stubble, grey
in late summer heat.
The road slows and stretches out;
a long black snake
basking in the morning sun.
Straight, the ride lulls us
to a meditative state.
Sheep so still, a quick
glance sees them stone;
small granite boulders nosing through
the lee side of the hill.

We drive
north to escape the sense
that standing still
is one foot out of six
beneath the ground.
Road side's littered with plaques
that mark the resting place
of towns half-remembered in
the double barreled names
of the district football teams –
Premiers '06,
'07 and '13.

We drive
north, the vista

never seems to change
but ruined farmsteads
claw up from the scrub;
each year sees them less
above ground than before.
Limestone monuments
forestalling the end of a dream.

We drive
north and the next
town feels just like
the one we left behind.
Familiar looks in faces
resigned to settling down.
Dusty streets, shrivelled
grass, young children marched
off to a school
that bears family names
on halls, fundraised
playground sets
and clay-brick memorials.

We drive on
and on, that long black snake
to feel it curve back
upon itself.

limestone ruins
seasoning the hillside
pepper trees

A Shepherd Mourning

He stands
alone, ghostly
white and at ease. A stiff
backed son of empire
he is not.

But there's a supple strength
that yields alike to drought
and flood,
that bends like barley
to the wind
but does not break.

His rifle's held barrel end;
a walking stick
to conquer wheat-sown,
sheep-trod hills.

A fresh faced farm lad
he was. I half expect
a stalk of wheat
behind his ear
or his slouch hat
tipped back
and to hear him talk of rain.

No blast
of bugle rudely blown
will rouse this lad

from marbled sleep. He waits
for heaven's trumpet call
to march.

Until that final reveille
he stands
on watch with garlands
at his feet.
A shepherd mourning
...for lost sheep.

Airport Lounge Remembrance
after Wilfred Owen's Send Off

A few, a few, too few for drums and yells,
they pass us by
in airport lounges, off to foreign hells.

Their camouflage no more dispels
the seeking eye,

so common to our life they fade in sight.
They come and go
like fatigued FIFO workers day and night;
partners waiting for their safe return, might
be the only show.

No protest march, no ticker tape parade.
For some silence.
Slow news days provoke a story; clichéd
right down to myth and mateship. A charade
at their expense.

A death will drop the flag to half mast.
To suit their cause
politicians evoke conflict a century past.
We'll dredge up some connection, eyes downcast.
Some will pause

and think of airport lounges, passers by.
A few, too few, will remember why.

Magpie Tales

outliving the town
        the gravestones at Keilli

Lest We Forget
after reading The Forgotten War

"Teach them a lesson
they'll never forget. Hang them
high as a warning to the rest
of those black bastards."

Teach them the worth
of a side of beef
in women, children,
men, deceased.

Teach them the arbitrary
arm of the law, one
white man worth one
hundred or more
black souls running
through the bush –
bullet holes in the back
of their charred remains.

It's there in white
and black, as if nothing
was wrong – ad hoc campaigns
over long, long years.

Teach them the lesson
they'll never forget.
Hang them high
as a warning to the rest.

Because
forgetting...
forgetting's
what us whitefellas
do best.

two men argue
                about the burqa ban -

she feeds the blackbirds

Those Country Towns
after Kenneth Slessor

A wide street, not for bullock trains
to turn, instead a track
for horse drawn trains carting grain
down from foothills to the port.

The general store died; rose
again – a wood fired pizza
shop, now restaurant, serving
city fare at city prices.

Prices ran the bakery,
matched Hogans for industry
but bread hasn't baked here
since the eighties. Time and money
saved trucking it in, no sense
competing with below cost bread.

Farmers drive fat bodied utes
to towns that were two days ride
away. Pay tribute to the one
armed kings; drown their suffering.

An Art Deco hall replaced
the Institute, vaudeville
troupes, sporadic, still pass through but
insurance killed community
arts, along with the flat screen
and cheap, streamed entertainment.

The football team paints the town
red and white and nothing's said –
just locals grasping a shred
of hometown pride before jobs or
joblessness draw them south
to bright lights and promises.

This town's placed its bet on dreams
of city feet escaping
the press and rush of uptight
life, to doze till three or four,
and play knee deep
in the rip free bay.

Only to hear complaints
about heat, flies, mosquitoes,
the lack of shops and free Wi-Fi.

old farm midden
digging through broken history
an empty bottle
still carries a message
from the hand that tossed it

A Rural Mythology

Bronzed Adonis - envy of every man;
John played full forward for the district, seemed
to have that golden touch; women preened
moth-drawn, eager to catch his hand.
It was assumed by most he'd take his chance
at the big league, then - wife, kids, that dream
we're told we dream. But things not always being
what they are, transmuted thoughts of romance
to lead; broke hearts by leaving town to search;
for something - he couldn't say. Thought it best
to go. Came back at his dying Mum's request -
still golden as she slipped into the church
long straight hair, red lips and a sleek black dress -
now Joanne, transformed; a modern goddess.

Wild Dogs Dreaming

The King

Sun Wukong
was my first
superhero.

No journalist Jesus
with his undies
on the outside.

No dark defender
of Gotham's
status quo.

It was . . .

philosophy lite
on a weekday
afternoon.

Twirling

a broomstick
to a seventies
pop tune.

His journey
to the west
gave us cloud surfing
and Buddhism

...before Tenzin.

He was a larrikin
in yellow skin

before chip shop owners
and card playing
brought us to hating
those like
him.

It didn't matter
back then;
the colour of his skin.

He was irrepressible,
the King.

morning chill –
    a scorpion salutes the sun

Lucilia Cuprina - an ode.

first beat of spring
careening down chimney
full bore into wall,
window pane, again
again.

daylight moth snared
by sun – carry on in vain
til spent; flaring,
failing filament
in backstroked spasms
on the sill

silent.

life erupts
wriggling free from
bulbous husk,
such plenty that one
might fall,
find some scrap or
cat food bowl.

there.
all life; death
in one space.
all lessons
in its maligned
embrace.

First Carvings
after Lynne Kelly

There's something beyond
this physical act;
deft scooped cuts
on roughed out wood.

Something more
that draws me in
beyond the pain
of fingers clawed
from work with
grain and form.

Revelation
at my own hand?
Or whispers
of the once living;
a daemon calling
in candlelight?

*You shall not make
a graven form -*
echo of a time before
when memory walked
wood and land;
danced and sang
the names of stone.

There's something

at the degree
of blood,
of bone;
something
that feels
like walking
home.

blistered hand
　　　I dig with my pen instead

Wild Dogs Dreaming

Ranges cut our town in two
from east to west – an ancient
ochre monolith, toppled
and crumbling on its side.

In that flat space of youth
they could be seen from any spot
we stood. Transmission towers
on the tallest one, let us fix

how far and in what direction
we'd gone. Our final year
before moving on, we took
the switch-back access road,

joked of adventures to come;
five teens half-paralyzed with fear
of the unknown. And standing on the rusted
launch where hang gliders would drop

and catch the desert air, we cupped
the cradle of our lives in one hand,
watched it flicker and burn through the night.
At dawn returned, convinced we had a plan.

A Fox Thought
for Sylvia

A momentary glimpse
of road and ditch:
the fox is dead,
the body crushed,
save for the snout
and head, mouth fixed
in an elliptical "oh",
as if caught by surprise
or uttering a warning cry.

Passing: a flash of red
and the fox thought jumps
to her death; the stink
of gas; the final mask
of her features - lips
rounded in expulsion
of relief or pursed
for a final appeal
at belief.

The Bull and the China pieces

Falling. Slow motion, one
second riding high; Godlike
on the back of a horned beast,
the next it plants, kicks quicker
than the eye can catch. But blood
knows.
       Blood sounds the warning gong
as everything fractures; fine
hairline cracks on the inside
of a bone china cup.
              Look
up; count back from one hundred
in sevens, logic over
exact calculation. Keep
moving down the list till
what's broken is found. Sometimes
nothing can be done – patience,
time.
       Godhood's a delusion –
I'm the rampaging beast,
and the china pieces
in one.

Confusion and Showgirl Tunes

On weekends our small band would head on bikes
to that jut of bush in the wash of new developments.
There were rocks, spinifex,
resurrection ferns and a giant fig
sprouting between a bouldered outcrop –
a Mount Diogenes in miniature.

We'd run along weathered paths, play soldiers
or capture the flag; til that summer we found
a girlie mag left by some other gang of boys.
You hooted and jeered; over the top. Embarrassed
and flushed, all I remember was her lush
permed hair – it was the eighties. Then later

that night in your pool, I was confused
and not only by your love of showgirl tunes.

Unguarded

My mother couldn't abide
the smell of pine incense.
Pleaded that it reminded her
of the cloying cleanliness
of her own mother's funeral.

Petulant; I hadn't experienced
memory's stealthy crawl
and pounce; the cruel bite
of remembrance.

Nor how memory can be
endowed through talk and thought –
so this unguarded walk
under murmuring pines
carries a sadness
trebled over time.

eating twilight shadows in the koi pond

Notes

That Summer - Published in *Adelaide InDaily,* November 6th, 2013 and subsequently in the inaugural edition of *Writ. Poetry Review*, September 30th, 2014.

Crossroads - Published in *Poetry and Place Anthology 2015*, April 2016.

Black Snake Driving - Published on *Bluepepper*, 23 February, 2016.

A Shepherd Mourning - Published in *Tincture Journal* Issue 8, December 2014. This poem began as a Shakespearean sonnet.

Airport Lounge Remembrance - Published in *Eureka Street* April 2015.

Lest We Forget - Published in *Pressure Gauge Journal*, Issue 1. The quotation that begins this poem is a combination of two newspaper quotes from early Australian newspapers that I overheard on Radio National. The wording has only been altered for rhythm.

old farm midden - Published in *Poetry and Place Anthology 2015*, April 2016.

Rural Mythology - The acceptance of LGBTI+ folk in rural areas is fraught, and particularly harsh for trans people. I wanted to be true to that experience of a trans person having to hide their true self and to move away for acceptance.

In titling the poem *Rural Mythology* I wanted it to be both an admission that the scenario that plays out is perhaps not yet a reality and thus myth and not true, but to also offer a sense of hope in terms of myth shaping and directing a possible future. That and of course the power of gods to transform their shape.

The King - Published in *Tincture Journal* Issue. 5, March 2014. I honestly thought I might have to explain who the racist chip shop owner was. Unfortunately, she got into parliament again.

Morning Chill - Published in *A Hundred Gourds Journal*, September 2014.

Lucilla Cuprina - Published at *Verity La*, April 13, 2017

First Carvings - This poem is a product at my first attempts at wood carving and having read Lynne Kelly's thesis in popular fiction form, *The Memory Code*.

blistered - I was reading Heaney's *Digging* at the time of composing this Haiku.

Wild Dogs Dreaming - Alhekulyele is the Arrernte name of Mount Gillen in Central Australia, which this poem takes place on. The area is associated with *Wild Dog Dreaming* stories. The title is intended as a nod to the Arrernte people, traditional owners of Mparntwe (Alice Springs).

A Fox Thought - The title is a play on Ted Hughes', *The Thought Fox*. The poem was triggered by an encounter with a real fox and a reading of Emily Van Duyne's article, *Why Are We So Unwilling to Take Sylvia Plath at Her Word?*

The Bull and The China Pieces - Published in *SNAP Literary Journal*, August 2016.

Confusion and Showgirl Tunes - Published in *Tincture Journal*, Issue 15, September 2016.

Unguarded - Published on *Bluepepper*, 2nd November, 2016.

www.ingramcontent.com/pod-product-compliance
Lightning Source LLC
Chambersburg PA
CBHW020704300426
44112CB00007B/506